HOW TO K

HOW TO KNOW GOD'S WILL

DEREK CLEAVE

EVANGELICAL PRESS

EVANGELICAL PRESS
16/18 High Street, Welwyn, Herts. AL6 9EQ, England.

© Evangelical Press 1985

This edition first published by
Evangelical Press 1985

ISBN 0 85234 200 4

The basis of this book was previously published under
the title 'Follow my Leader'.

All Scripture references are taken from the New
International Version, Hodder and Stoughton, 1979.

Typeset by Inset, Chappel, Essex.
Printed in Great Britain by Cox & Wyman,
Reading, Berks.

Contents

Introduction

Introduction

During my ministry I have had the great
privilege of working with young people. I have
also been a young person myself!

I therefore know something of the difficulties
which young Christians in particular have over
the important matter of guidance. I have spent
hours talking with them and this subject has
been raised and discussed many times. Having
'done their own thing' in their pre-Christian days
they are now concerned to do the 'right thing'.

I felt that a series of studies on knowing and
doing the will of God would be helpful, though
I don't claim to be an 'expert' in either field.
It is a subject in which we are all learners, but
the Scriptures do provide us with clear principles
to follow. These studies were originally given a
few years ago at various young people's house-

parties, and the substance of that series is now here in a more permanent form.

I trust that it will reach and help a wider audience of young people and perhaps even some who are 'not so young', but who want to know and do God's will.

Derek Cleave

1.
Why should I?
The will of God and its importance

1.
Why should I?
The will of God and its importance

The most important thing in anyone's life is to know the will of God and to follow it.

If we accept the fact that God is the Supreme Being then there can be nothing more important than obeying his will for our lives. Man would not exist, were it not for the will of God. Since we do exist, then we exist for a purpose because a wise God is not going to involve himself in purposeless creation. That purpose is the will of God for your life and mine. It is different for each of us but equally important to all of us.

This is where we have to begin, because my attitude to God and his will and purpose for my life is the deciding factor as to the quality of my relationship with him in time and in eternity.

A child who ignores his parents' wishes places himself at odds with them and could be in for a rough ride! The same thing, but with far more serious consequences, will be the result of a 'couldn't-care-less' attitude to our heavenly Father. It is this difference in attitude which should distinguish the believer from the un-believer, the Christian from the non-Christian.

Rejection of the will of God by our first parents brought sin into the world with its awful consequences. Almost at the beginning of the Bible and early in man's existence we read, 'Everyone did as *he* saw fit' (Judges 17:6). That attitude has been with mankind now through thousands of years. We are born *with* it, and the multiplicity of problems we experience are 'born' *from* it. The Bible can sum up the human dilemma in one sentence and by using a picture that is not entirely complimentary when it says, 'We all, like sheep, have gone astray, each of us has turned to *his own way*' (Isaiah 53:6).

I can illustrate the point in this way. The maker of my car has suggested what octane fuel I should use, but he doesn't accompany me to every garage to make sure that I follow his instructions! Having given the advice, he leaves me to follow it. If I refuse to pay for a particular grade and consistently buy the cheaper fuel, that is my responsibility. But if I then experience problems in the running of my car, I dare not go back to the maker and complain. I chose not to follow his instructions; I must now accept the consequences. When the Bible tells us that we have 'gone astray' it is stating a fact and we must accept any responsibility for ignoring the Maker's instructions. If God *is* the Creator and we are the creatures, then it is his right to make the rules.

Man's problems, *our* problems, exist largely because of a conflict of nature between man and God — the created and the Creator.

How thankful we should be, therefore, that, through his Son Jesus Christ, God is able to break the stranglehold that 'self' has in our lives! The radical difference in the life of the Christian believer is that it is now *possible* for his will to be in harmony with the will of God.

Perhaps you are saying at this point, 'But I accept the importance of the will of God in my life. Let's get on with how I can find out what it is.' Wait just for a moment. We may accept it in principle, but do we really appreciate *why* it is important? Let's lay a good foundation to build on in later chapters. There are three reasons we are going to identify as to why the will of God is important in our lives, but before we come to them one further point must be made.

In defining the subject, the Bible refers to both a 'secret' will of God and a 'revealed' will of God. Deuteronomy 29:29 tells us that 'The secret things belong to the Lord our God.' This means that there are certain things which God knows that we do not know and perhaps will never know. He has not chosen to reveal them to us, since they belong to his 'secret' will. There are, however, other matters which God has revealed and is revealing; in these he expects our obedience. It is therefore the *revealed* will of God that we are concerned with in the following chapters.

Remember, throughout your reading of this book, that our obedience to the will of God is primarily for his glory, and only secondarily for our benefit.

Now let's look in more detail at three reasons for its importance.

1. Our duty to God

There are only two parties involved in this relationship — God and man. Let's consider God first.

God — the Creator

In the Bible the sovereignty of God is strongly emphasized. He is seen as the Creator and his will as the cause of all things. As well as the account of creation in Genesis, the following examples will clearly confirm this. The Bible tells us that 'By the word of the Lord were the heavens made, their starry host by the breath of his mouth . . . he spoke, and it came to be; he commanded, and it stood firm' (Psalm 33:6,9).

The Bible also informs us that 'The Lord is the great God, the great King above all gods. In his hand are the depths of the earth, and the mountain peaks belong to him. The sea is his, for he made it, and his hands formed the dry land. Come, let us bow down in worship, let us kneel before the Lord our Maker; for he is our God' (Psalm 95:3—7).

The account of creation shows us that when God made the world he did it with 'a word', whereas when a man 'creates' he needs materials, tools and workmen. God creates by his sovereign power with 'a word' and from nothing!

Part of this creation is man — initially the summit of God's work, yet made from dust, which itself was made from nothing at all! Any boasting on our part, therefore, is surely out of place! It would be fitting for man to glory or 'boast' in the fact that he is part of God's wonderful creation, whereas his fallen and sinful nature tempts him to deny this and in so doing to deny God himself. The Bible shows that this is an illogical position to take and brands the man who does so as 'a fool' (Psalm 14:1; 53:1). In the New Testament, Paul reminds us that 'Since the creation of the world God's invisible qualities — his eternal power and divine nature — have been clearly seen, being understood from what has been made, so that men are without any excuse' (Romans 1:20).

This situation produces a problem for self-centred man. If there is a Being who made him then that Being is superior to him, and is someone to whom he is answerable. But man's independence doesn't want to be answerable to anyone, and one of the ways to deal with that 'problem' is to 'dispose' of God. Not everyone adopts that attitude, of course, though the God of the Bible is not popular today, even among some people who 'believe' in him. Their 'belief' exists so long as God makes no demands on them.

God — the Upholder
But to go a little further, this Sovereign God

18

not only creates; he upholds. Though God is self-sufficient, man is not. Paul, when speaking to the philosophers in Athens and contrasting their dead gods with the Creator God, points out that it is 'in him we live and move and have our being' (Acts 17:28). The very next breath we draw is God-given and if he were to choose to deprive us of it, then there is nothing that we, or a thousand doctors, could do to reverse it. And what about the food which is necessary to fuel our bodies? God is the one who provides it. 'The eyes of all look to you, and you give them their food at the proper time. You open your hand and satisfy the desires of every living thing' (Psalm 145:15,16). We labour to produce food of various kinds, yet even in the growing of what we eat there is that which God does which we cannot understand or imitate.

> We plough the fields and scatter
> The good seed on the ground,
> *But it is fed and watered*
> *By God's almighty hand.*

God is, therefore, not only our Creator, but also our Upholder and consequently the Bible shows us that everything in the world belongs

to him. He is 'the Creator (Possessor) of heaven
and earth' (Genesis 14:19). We are told, 'To
the Lord your God belong the heavens, even
the highest heavens, the earth and everything
in it' (Deuteronomy 10:14). Surely the only
honest position to take is the one that expresses
debt and gratitude to this sovereign God.

But the other half of the relationship is
man, created innocent, but spoilt through
disobedience to God's will.

Man and his failure

We had already begun to look at ourselves in
the introduction to this chapter. Man's failure
in the beginning was voluntary because he had
a will which of itself was sufficient to repel
the temptation. The devil didn't have the power
to force him to disobey. Thomas Watson
reminds us that 'The devil was a suitor to woo,
not a king to compel.' But man at his best
failed and, contrary to what some might try
to tell us, far from his having improved with
the passage of time and become more respon-
sible, the evidence suggests that man is less
capable of making the right choice today than
he was then. His entire nature has now been
corrupted because of the influence of sin. Yet
because men are so proud we invariably trust

our own judgement rather than obey God's will.

John Newton, the preacher and hymn writer of the eighteenth century, wrote the following words, which illustrate what utter failures we would be if left to ourselves:

Once upon a time, a paper kite
Mounted to a wondrous height,
Where, giddy with its elevation,
It thus expressed self-admiration:
'See how the crowds of gazing people
Admire my flight above the steeple!

How they would wonder if they knew
All that a kite like me can do!
Were I but free, I'd take a flight
And pierce the clouds beyond their sight;
But, ah! Like a poor prisoner bound,
My string confines me to the ground!

I'd brave the eagle's towering wing
Might I but fly without the string.'
It tugged and pulled while thus it spoke —
To snap the string; at last it broke.
Deprived at once of all its stay,
In vain it tried to soar away:

Unable its own weight to bear,
It fluttered downward through the air;
Unable its own course to guide,
The wind soon plunged it in the tide.
Ah! Foolish kite, thou hast no wing;
How couldst thou fly without a string?

My heart cried out, 'Oh, Lord, I see
How much this kite resembles me!
Forgetful that by Thee I stand,
Impatient of Thy ruling hand;

How oft I've wished to break the lines
Thy wisdom for my lot assigns,
How oft indulge the vain desire
For something more, or something higher!
But for Thy grace and love divine,
A fall this dreadful had been mine!'

Notice, then, that even in the Christian the old independence rears its ugly head.

The hymn writer William Williams, composing at about the same time as John Newton, put into words what should be the perfect relationship between God and man:

Guide me, O thou great Jehovah,
Pilgrim through this barren land;
I am weak but Thou art mighty,
Hold me with Thy powerful hand.

Each living being owes its existence to God; therefore every man ought to express his debt of gratitude by freely doing the will of God. By nature, however, we are utterly incapable of doing this. By nature we want to remain independent of God, making our own decisions, deciding our own fate. This is the very essence of sin and is the reason why continuing disobedience to the will of God is the characteristic of the person who is not a follower of Christ.

Man — and the new birth

Our only answer is to receive a new nature, a God-orientated nature. Only God himself can provide this through the miracle of the new birth, which makes us willing to renounce our self-centred nature. This then produces a life that experiences fulfilment and satisfaction in doing the will of God. From that moment of new birth (see John 3), we have the potential to begin to fulfil the true purpose of our creation. The apostle Paul, towards the end of

23

his ministry, was giving testimony to the miracle that God had performed in his life and referred to the words of Ananias spoken to him at the time: 'The God of our fathers has chosen you to know his will' (Acts 22:14). From that moment Paul's motivations were entirely changed. His primary concern was to do the will of God, and in this he was exhibiting one of the distinguishing marks of the true Christian believer. When writing to the Christians in Rome, he told them, 'If we live, we live to the Lord; and if we die, we die to the Lord. So, whether we live or die, we belong to the Lord' (Romans 14:8). He expressed a similar truth when he told the Corinthians that 'He [Jesus] died for all, that those who live should no longer live for themselves but for him who died for them and was raised again' (2 Corinthians 5:15).

Paul would certainly have been happy to associate himself with these words from Darley Terry:

> The Lord is King! I own His power,
> His right to rule each day and hour;
> I own His claim on heart and will,
> And His demands I would fulfil.

He would also have been prepared to under-line the warning of these words from Josiah Conder:

> The Lord is King! Who then shall dare
> Resist His will, distrust His care,
> Or murmur at His wise decrees,
> Or doubt His royal promises?

Let us now consider another reason why the will of God is important.

2. Our devotion to Christ

Obeying God's will is nothing less than our duty to him, but it is also an expression of our devotion to the Lord Jesus Christ.

Some of the most remarkable chapters in the New Testament record the conversations between Jesus and his disciples just before the crucifixion. Much of this is found in the Gospel of John, in chapters 13—16. During the discourse Jesus refers to the greatest expression of love that one man can have for another: 'Greater love has no one than this,

25

that one lay down his life for his friends' (John 15:13). Within hours Jesus was going to prove his love for them and us in doing that very thing. Notice that he has referred to us as his friends, yet when he died men had not shown him any of the fruits of friendship. Paul tells us that at the very moment when Christ died for us 'we were still powerless' and 'ungodly', and, most graphically of all, 'we were God's enemies', but 'God demonstrates his own love for us in this: While we were still sinners, Christ died for us' (Romans 5:6,8,10). Now to his followers Jesus said, 'You are my friends *if you do what I command*' (John 15:14). Here is an important reason for being concerned about obedience to the will of God. There is both reassurance and responsibility emphasized here, for one depends on the other. We can be absolutely sure that we are the friends of Jesus Christ if we do what he commands. Jesus wanted to make this absolutely clear to his disciples, so he gave them a remarkable parallel: 'If you obey my commands, you will remain in my love, just as I have obeyed my Father's commands and remain in his love' (John 15:10).

Therefore our obedience to the will of God in Christ is proof of our love for him. We dare not adopt a casual attitude to this subject. Every time the will of God confronts us, our attitude to it will reveal our devotion to Christ, or otherwise! In the light of this it doesn't matter as much what we say in our devotions or how hard we work in Christian service; the question we must ask ourselves is this: 'How promptly and how perfectly do I obey the will of God?' That is the ultimate test.

But this is not the only occasion where Jesus makes clear this test of love. Mark records the fact that on one occasion Jesus was speaking in a house when his mother and brothers arrived. They remained outside but sent someone in to call Jesus. When Jesus was informed that his mother and brothers were outside looking for him he said, 'Who are my mother and my brothers? . . . Whoever does God's will is my brother and sister and mother' (Mark 3:33,35).

Here obedience to the will of God does not merely express friendship with Christ, but a relationship which is even closer! There is, of course, no lack of affection between the Lord and his earthly relatives, but he is taking the opportunity to make clear to the people who are listening to him that the relationship with his disciples and his followers is a different and, in fact, a more sacred tie. Only those who recognize the work and the will of the Son of God could really be considered his brother and sister and mother. Here was the primary purpose of his coming to this earth, in order to bring people into the family of God — his family — so that they might know and obey the will of his Father, just as he did. Even the Lord's earthly relatives could not break in upon his ministry just because of the human relationship that existed between them.

The people who are in the closest possible relationship to Jesus Christ the Son of God are those who are obedient to his will. This is an immense privilege and this relationship, close though it may be, is not to be treated flippantly or casually. He is still God and we are only men. We can never be on 'familiar' terms with him. Paul confirms this in writing to the Ephesians when he suggests that they are 'like slaves of Christ, doing the will of God from your heart' (Ephesians 6:6). It is the heart of love that prompts obedience to his commands.

> My very best for Jesus is the least that
> I can do,
> And in His service I will bring my steadfast
> love and true,
> For all that I can render is not half that is
> His due,
> So help me, Lord, to honour Thee in all
> that I pursue.

There is also a third reason why the will of God is important.

3. Our desire for the world

How many times have you prayed, 'Thy will be done on earth, as it is in heaven'? Obviously more times than can easily be counted, since this phrase is a part of what we call 'the Lord's Prayer'. Actually it was a model prayer which Jesus gave to his disciples, and not a prayer that he himself would pray. Therefore it has also been referred to as 'the Disciples' Prayer' or 'the Family Prayer'. Both of these titles are perfectly correct since they imply that prayer can only be offered in reality by those who are in the family of God, i.e. children of God who have every right to call him Father, and so those who are disciples of the Lord Jesus Christ.

It is hypocritical for an unbeliever to recite this prayer, because his very position is a contradiction of it. He himself is one of those refusing to do the will of God on earth and he will continue in this state until he steps into the will of God, repenting of his sinful disobedience and putting faith in his Son. Those who have become God's children here on earth pray that

God's will might be done on earth *now*, as it is so perfectly performed in heaven. That should be the desire of everyone whose nature has been changed and who can therefore truly pray this from the heart.

But just a moment! It is one thing for a believer to *pray* this prayer; it is another thing for that same believer to endeavour to make that prayer *true* in his or her life. It would be wrong for us to suggest that the unbeliever's rejection of God's will makes it a mockery for him to pray the prayer, if we, as believers, also hesitate to obey him! And, just as important, our failure to obey will hinder the effectiveness of our lives as a witness to others. It is primarily as men see the will of God being obeyed in the lives of those who *are* God's children that they themselves will be influenced. People are challenged by the Christian faith as they see it operating in another person's life. The proclamation of the gospel message should always be confirmed by the evidence of changed lives. The unconverted are not challenged by gimmicks or novelties.

We have often heard people bear witness to the fact that their interest in Christianity was initiated because of the challenge that a certain Christian's life was to them. At the time the unbeliever could not have identified what it was, but it was something which made the Christian quite different from everyone else, and above all it was attractive. What was it? The well-known Methodist preacher, Dr W. E. Sangster, said, 'A holy life is still the greatest evangelistic agency in the whole world.' We know that part of God's revealed will for us as believers is that we should be holy. It has rightly been emphasized that 'God saved us to make us holy, not to make us happy.' That is the correct balance. The more holy we become, the happier we shall be, but happiness is the by-product, not the purpose. Holiness is the purpose of our salvation.

The apostle Peter tells us that 'Just as he who called you is holy, so be holy in all you do; for it is written, "Be holy, because I am holy"' (1 Peter 1:15,16). Obedience to this command from God will always have repercussions in an unholy world.

Others have remarked that their interest in Christianity was fostered because a certain person showed love, concern and compassion when others were too involved in their own selfish pursuits. That 'certain person' happened to be a Christian obeying the new commandment which Jesus gave to his disciples, and therefore to us, that we should love each other as a witness to the world: 'A new commandment I give you: Love one another. As I have loved

31

you, so you must love one another. All men will know that you are my disciples if you love one another' (John 13:34,35). Here again we shall see obedience to the revealed will of God bearing fruit.

Do you now see that the will of God being actively followed in our lives as Christian believers is *the* key to reaching men and women for Christ? The best way to get others to do the will of God and so to help answer the prayer, 'Thy will be done on earth as it is in heaven,' is not only to pray the prayer but to make sure that we are doing it ourselves!

In the light of these three reasons we dare not adopt a casual attitude to the claims of God on our lives as members of his family.

Firstly, he is our Creator, our Provider and our Redeemer, and it is a glorious duty for us to be able to do the will of God 'from the heart'.

Secondly, Jesus Christ is our Saviour and Lord and this relationship to him will be tested by our readiness to do his will.

Thirdly, as Christians we desire to see 'heaven on earth' in the matter of the world's obedience to the will of God. We must realize, then, that as Christians, *our* obedience to that very same will has repercussions in a world that does not naturally know and do God's will.

2.
Better than precept
The will of God and the example of Christ

2.
Better than precept
The will of God and the example of Christ

We are told that 'An ounce of practice is worth a pound of preaching', because men are imitators by nature, which only goes to prove that example can be better than precept. There are always those who look to us for an example — perhaps a younger brother or sister, our own children, or just people who respect us for one reason or another. Therefore example *is* important.

God has acknowledged this fact, since he has provided us with the finest possible example for every area of life. In Jesus Christ, his own Son, we have one who said, 'I seek not to please myself but him who sent me' (John 5:30). Jesus did nothing without the agreement and the authority of his Father. Unlike mankind in general, he never acted independently. He lived

a life of perfect obedience to the will of his
Father.

As believers we are 'followers' of Jesus Christ;
we look to him as our Leader and find that we
can have no better example for every aspect of
our Christian life. However, to look at the
example of Christ and the way in which he
obeyed the will of his Father must not be
viewed merely as a theological exercise, nor
even serve only as an inspiration to us, but
rather it must be a duty to be obeyed. John
reminds us that 'Whoever claims to live in him
must walk as Jesus did' (1 John 2:6). The word
'walk' here means to 'live in the same way',
and we *must* do it.

It was never an imposition for Jesus Christ to
do the will of his Father. There was, and is,
a perfect union existing between Father and
Son. Notice again that Jesus said, 'I seek not to
please myself but [I seek to please] him who
sent me.' Do you see his *attitude*? So the
attitude of our obedience will be important to
God. In my own family, my children must obey
me because I am their father. I believe that
the instructions which I give them stem from
love, and are for their good, and it is their duty
to obey me (see Ephesians 6:1). But it is far
better if they obey me because they love me and
believe that the course of action I require is for

their good. It is, therefore, of supreme importance that we obey God, who is our heavenly Father; but it is a great delight to God if we obey him willingly because we believe that what he requires from us is for our ultimate good. This presupposes that commands should be reasonable, that is, there should be a reason for them and a purpose behind them. There must have been reasons for Christ to do the will of his Father and we will look at these as we consider his example.

1. Fulfilment

Uppermost in the mind of Jesus Christ at all times was the fact that he was fulfilling a plan. Throughout his life he was utterly consistent in this objective. We read of him as a pre-teenager discussing theological issues with the religious teachers of the day. When his parents eventually discovered him, they could not understand how Jesus could have treated them in this way. Jesus immediately asked the question: 'Why were you searching for me? Didn't you know I had to be in my Father's house?' (Luke 2:49). Throughout his ministry he referred to the fact that '[his] time [had] not yet come' (John 2:4; 7:30; 8:20) and then, just prior to the most awful death to confront any man, he again acknowledged his submission to the will of his Father as he prayed in the garden of Gethsemane: 'Father, if you are will-ing, take this cup from me; yet not my will, but yours be done' (Luke 22:42).

The fact that Jesus did the will of his Father does not suggest that his own judgement would have been wrong, but it does show us that Jesus had no private aims. He did not come to this earth to promote his own ideas or to make something of himself for his own ends. His one objective was to do the will of his Father.

He made this absolutely clear when he said, 'I have come down from heaven not to do my will but to do the will of him who sent me' (John 6:38). Jesus tells us here that he 'came down *from* heaven'. In verse 33 he tells these people that 'The bread of God is he who comes down from heaven and gives life to the world.' Then in verse 35 he declares, 'I am the bread of life. He who comes to me will never go hungry, and he who believes in me will never be thirsty,' and when we come to verse 40 there is a clear statement of the fact that he is the Son of God. For this reason alone we must surely trust his word when he tells us that he did not come to do his own will, but the will of his Father. He had every intention that the Father's purposes should be worked out through him and nothing was going to hinder him in fulfilling his Father's will. Again we should emphasize that there was never a moment when this was an imposition upon Jesus. Thousands of years before the coming of Christ the psalmist wrote prophetic words expressing the attitude of the Messiah to the work which God had given him to do: 'To do your will, O my God, is my desire' (Psalm 40:8). It was his greatest wish. Even when the life of Jesus was taken from him, he was not an unwilling sacrifice. He spoke of 'laying down his life' for men (John 10:15—17) and the message of the New Testament is that Jesus Christ, the Son of God, died voluntarily because he loved us. He tells us that it was impossible for anyone else to take his life from him: 'I lay it down of my own accord' (John 10:18). He was the only one with power over his life, both to give it and to take it again. In the fulfilment of his Father's will, with which he was in complete agreement, he *'gave'* his life for us!

When Christ eventually cried out, 'It is finished!' this was not a cry of defeat, or even relief, but a cry of triumph, in that against all the powers of evil set against him, he had triumphed in doing the will of his Father.

39

Can you now see that through the obedience of Christ to the will of his Father the way has been provided for our sinful independence to be forgiven and forgotten? But more than that: a reborn man now has the potential to fulfil the will of God during his lifetime! So, in a similar way to Christ himself, we should obey the will of God since we now have a plan to follow and fulfil.

Wise creators usually have a purpose in mind for their creation. Certainly everything God makes, he makes for a purpose. Jesus illustrates that it is possible for us, as his followers and as children of God, to have no higher aim in life than a desire to do the will of our heavenly Father. But there was something more. We will now look at a second reason for the obedience of Christ.

2. Fellowship

In the conversation between Jesus and his disciples just prior to his death, he said to them: 'If you obey my commands, you will remain in my love, just as I have obeyed my Father's commands and remain in his love' (John 15:10). Here Jesus is looking back upon an entire life of obedience when he says, 'I have obeyed.' He uses the tense which reaches from the past and has a significance for the present, giving the sense of 'Because I have obeyed, I am forever remaining in his love.' The relationship between God the Father and God the Son was a never-ending circle of love and obedience. The Son loved the Father and therefore obeyed the Father's commands, and because the Son obeyed the Father's commands the Father loved him. Love prompted obedience and obedience prompted love.

The depth of unity between the Father and the Son was never more clearly seen than when Jesus had said, 'The reason my Father loves me is that I lay down my life — only to take it up again. No one takes it from me, but I lay it down of my own accord. I have authority to lay it down and authority to take it up again. This command I received from my Father' (John 10:17,18). As we saw earlier, Jesus is saying here that no one is able to take his life away from him, but he gives it up of his own accord. Because of who he is, he has the right to lay it down and he has the right to take it again. But notice that he can also add, 'This *command* I received from my Father.' Obedience and love live together.

Later the apostle Paul is able to say of Jesus

that he 'became obedient to death' (Philippians 2:8). He alone could be in that position. If his life had been taken forcibly from him, then he would not have given it and that would have made it victory for his captors and defeat for him. The Father therefore loves him because of his voluntary giving up of life in accordance with his will. There was complete unanimity, and this must be accepted for a right understanding of the Scriptures. Some have suggested, quite wrongly, that there is a gulf between the character of the Father and of the Son. On one hand, they say, we have an angry Judge and on the other a loving Saviour. The Bible does not confirm that dichotomy. Jesus could look to the cross as an accomplished fact before it happened and say, 'I have brought you glory on earth by completing the work you gave me to do' (John 17:4). It was his Father's mission in which he was in full agreement. There was perfect communion throughout the whole of his life. Look at these further examples from John's Gospel:

'I tell you the truth, the Son can do nothing by himself; he can do only what he sees his Father doing, because whatever the Father does the Son also does. For the

Father loves the Son and shows him all he does' (John 5:19,20).

'My teaching is not my own. It comes from him who sent me. If anyone chooses to do God's will, he will find out whether my teaching comes from God or whether I speak on my own' (John 7:16,17).

'The one who sent me is with me; he has not left me alone, for I always do what pleases him' (John 8:29).

Jesus claims absolute equality with his Father, yet shows his perfect submission to the will of his Father. These verses are only a sample of many instances where Jesus refers to the unity existing with his Father. All of this results in his remaining in his Father's love.

Now let's see how Jesus expresses the parallel in relation to his disciples and himself: 'If you obey my commands, you will remain in my love, *just as* I have obeyed my Father's commands and remain in his love' (John 15:10). It is obvious from this that obedience to his commands is evidence of our love for him and will ensure that we remain in his love. It is as true in our relationship with him as it was in his relationship with his Father.

Then let me show you a third aspect of our Lord's obedience to his Father.

3. The future

Jesus always had an eye to the future. The ninth chapter of John's Gospel records the story of a blind man who crossed his path. It is important to notice the difference in the reaction of Jesus and of his disciples. The disciples immediately ask Jesus, 'Rabbi, who sinned, this man or his parents, that he was born blind?' (v. 1) Jesus in replying states positively that there was something they could do to help the man. To the disciples it was a puzzle to be unravelled; to Jesus it was an opportunity to work. Then Jesus made this pertinent comment: 'As long as it is day, we must do the work of him who sent me. Night is coming, when no one can work' (v. 4). Here is another vital reason why Jesus obeyed his Father's will. Christ, the eternal Son of God, acknowledges here that his time as a man on earth is limited, for the reference to 'day' means his life, whereas the reference to 'night' is to death. But Jesus includes his disciples and therefore all his followers in the great commission because he says, '*We* must do the work of him who sent me.'

Jesus has but six months to live until he cries, 'It is finished!' He must make use of every opportunity. He says here of the blind man that 'This happened so that the work of God might be displayed in his life' (v. 3). This was to be a sign that would point men to Jesus and bring glory to God. He must therefore be obedient to the will of his Father, though it endangered his own life. The record tells us that it was the Sabbath and Jesus had narrowly escaped death once before for working on that day, but it was what he had been sent to do and he would not be detracted from it. Jesus had an eye to the future and realized that it was imperative to make use of every opportunity to do the will of his Father *now*. There would come a time when this avenue of service would be closed to him.

We need to be reminded of the urgency of the task that has been committed to us for 'As long as it is day, *we* must do the work of him who sent [us]. Night is coming, when no one can work,' and the 'night' comes for us all. In the Old Testament we are exhorted: 'Whatever your hand finds to do, do it with all your might, for in the grave, where you are going, there is neither working nor planning nor knowledge nor wisdom' (Ecclesiastes 9:10). We should, therefore, employ our time in doing the will of God. We only pass through this world once and we cannot return to correct errors or to make use of neglected opportunities.

> Only one life, 'twill soon be past,
> Only what's done for Christ will last.

How important it is for us to follow our Lord's example, because in the life of Christ we see the supreme example of obedience to the will of God! Fulfilment, fellowship and the future all had a part and in this he is our perfect Example. We must therefore walk in his footsteps for, 'Whoever claims to live in him must walk as Jesus did' (1 John 2:6).

There is one thing more. The Lord Jesus Christ himself walks with us! This has always been true of the relationship between God and his servants. When God sent Moses, he said to him, 'I will be with you' (Exodus 3:12). When Jesus sent out his disciples he said, 'Go [into the world] and make disciples of all nations . . . teaching them to obey everything I have commanded you. And surely I will be with you always, to the very end of the age' (Matthew 28:19,20). When God gives the commissioning, he always provides the enabling.

3.
Check list
The will of God and its characteristics

3.
Check list
The will of God and its characteristics

Are you afraid of the will of God? You might say, 'I don't want to be disobedient or reticent, but supposing he should ask me to do something that will hurt me?' That's why, at this point, we are going to look at the characteristics of the will of God. We are going to reassure ourselves that for harm to come to us is the last thing God wants for his children. I believe the apostle Paul can help us in this. He was a man who continually proved God in various situations and when he wrote to the Roman Christians he told them something that will encourage us.

In this magnificent epistle Paul moves from what is doctrinal (that is teaching) in the early chapters, to a series of practical exhortations. 'If you *believe this*, then *do this*.' In Romans 12 he begins by making a fervent appeal to his readers to make a complete dedication of their entire selves to the service of God. He points out that as Christians we should not copy the fleeting fashions of the present, but instead should be 'transformed by the renewing of [our] mind'. This transformation is the higher form of life which the believer now seeks to follow and is that life which is in conformity to the will of God. We have noticed already that this must be the characteristic of the believer when the opposite is true of the unbeliever.

With this 'renewed' mind we are able to view rightly the attributes and characteristics of the will of God. Without that transformation this would not be possible. We cannot rightly study and understand Christianity from outside. If I am thinking of purchasing a particular type of car, I am not going to consult a doctor as to its merits; I will speak to a mechanic. In a similar way, the renewed mind of the believer is the one best equipped to understand the will of God. Therefore Paul is able to say to these people, '*You* will be able to test and approve what God's will is — his good, pleasing and perfect will' (Romans 12:2). The word that is used for 'test' here is the word that is applied to the testing of metals by fire. It means to explore, to investigate, to discriminate and so to approve. And Paul says that our transformation will enable us to apply this rule to the characteristics of God's will. So let's use Paul's check list.

1. The will of God is good

The word that Paul uses here for 'good' emphasizes that all that is good is the will of God. Remember that it is only the renewed mind of the believer in harmony with God that can truly appreciate this. It is not for any man to decide what is good and then on this basis say that this is the will of God. The believer desires to have God's outlook and his renewed mind can therefore not only test that the will of God is good, but is also able to see that all that is good is the will of God. Let me illustrate this. Most people will acknowledge the fact that Jesus was a 'good' man. However, many of them mean that their knowledge of Jesus tells them he did those things which were helpful and kind to others, that is, 'good' things. However, when the believer says Jesus was 'a good man' he is meaning this in a far deeper sense. He is saying that Jesus was a 'good' man because he always and only did the will of God. His mind was one with his Father's. His appreciation of anything was God the Father's appreciation of that thing. His decisions were always in accord with his Father's will and there was always complete agreement between them.

It is important to notice in the Bible that two very basic words are used to describe that which is according to the will of God and that which is contrary to the will of God. The two words are 'good' and 'evil', and they are, of course, opposites. For example, Paul writing to the Romans says, 'There will be trouble and distress for every human being who does evil; . . . but glory, honour and peace for everyone who does good' (Romans 2:9,10). Again Paul writing to the Corinthians says that 'We must all appear before the judgement seat of Christ, that each one may receive what is due to him for the things done while in the body, whether good or bad' (2 Corinthians 5:10).

The point we are making here is the fact that the *only* thing which God can describe as 'good' is that which is according to his will. Anything else must therefore be disobedience and so evil or bad.

But what is the *message* of this word in connection with the will of God? The word used in relation to the will of God tells us quite clearly that God is the essence of goodness. There is even a link between the two English words 'God' and 'good'. For example, the word 'goodbye' is a contraction of 'God be with you'. So when Paul says that 'The will of God is good' it is a revelation of the character of God. If we read the Bible from the beginning we see God working unhindered and notice that without exception everything that God looks upon of his work is 'good'.

It is not possible for evil to emanate from God. That which he wills and does is always good. It might not appear so at the time and many without renewed minds would lay all manner of complaints at God's door.

Even Christians can be bewildered sometimes because we do not understand the circumstances and we only grasp the fact that the will of God is good simply because of what we know of the character and the trustworthiness of God. That giant of the Reformation, Martin Luther, once said, 'I know not the way God leads me, but well I know my guide.' It is sometimes a question of trusting where you cannot see, at least physically. Paul was able to say, 'We know that in all things God works for the good of those who love him, who have been called according to his purpose' (Romans

8:28). I love chocolate cake but I am sure that if I went to the kitchen when chocolate cake was being prepared and was offered a spoonful of dry flour or chocolate powder, a raw egg or a lump of butter, I wouldn't be able to enjoy any of those ingredients. People might then begin to doubt whether in fact I really did like chocolate cake. However, when all of these ingredients are mixed together and the cake is baked, then the cooked ingredients together are acceptable. It would be foolish, even for the Christian, to say that we enjoy every individual ingredient in life. But we are able to say, because of what we know of the character of God, that all of those individual events work *together* for good.

Pressures in life invariably bring resistance and rebellion from the unbeliever because he doesn't understand them. There are situations when a child will resist some action towards him which is for his ultimate good, simply because he doesn't understand why. As far as the believer is concerned, however, there need be no reticence in following the will of God. Do you see that it is bound to be good because of the character of its Originator? John Blanchard has written, 'Nothing good comes except from God, and nothing except good comes from God.' All this makes for a positive attitude to life. The Bible clearly shows that obedience to the will of God will bring us into something 'good'. It has rightly been said that the will of God 'is not a burden to carry; it is a pillow to rest on'.

2. The will of God is perfect

Here again the meaning of the word is important. In the Bible the word 'perfect' means 'faultless' or 'complete' and we must look at both shades of meaning.

God's will is faultless

The obvious answer as to why this must be so is rooted in the very character of God himself. He is perfection. He is without fault, therefore he cannot have a will with faults.

In our lives we are continually confronted with those things which are imperfect or defective. Household articles fall to pieces in our hands! Even mankind in general will acknowledge that 'We all have our faults!' But this is something that can never be attributed to God. Because of his nature, God cannot do anything which is less than perfect. Therefore

55

it is impossible for a mistake to be made which will harm or injure us, that is not for our ultimate good.

We must accept the fact that it is impossible for us to view events with God's perspective. It is in this situation that faith takes over from sight. Jesus himself once said to his Father, 'Yes Father, this was your good pleasure' (Luke 10:21). Jesus is praising his Father because certain things have been hidden from the wise and the clever and have been revealed to little children and he is expressing himself as being in harmony with the will of God. This is a lovely prayer of submission acknowledging the fact that it is his Father's view of things that is important. Remember that the man on the hilltop can always see more than the man in the valley.

Paul was one who was constantly proving the perfection of the will of God in his own life. In his second letter to the Corinthian Christians, he refers to 'a thorn in my flesh' (2 Corinthians 12:7). We are not sure what this was, but it could possibly have been a physical infirmity of some kind. Three times Paul had asked God to remove it and God had said that this was not to be so, but that his grace was sufficient for Paul in this particular trial. God knew best and it was not his will that the 'thorn' should be removed. Did Paul become despondent, or did he find fault because God had not answered his prayer? Did he allow someone to upset him by telling him that he did not have enough faith to be healed? No, he submitted himself to the will of God, acknowledging that there was a purpose in it. He proved that God's will is faultless.

God's will is complete

God does not live in time as we do. He does not therefore need to vary his will in any way. He makes his plans and carries them through. For example, in the matter of man's redemption Jesus could be spoken of as 'the Lamb that was slain from the creation of the world' (Revelation 13:8). God made his decision in eternity past and acted on it in a perfect and complete way. It is impossible for anyone to improve on God's way of doing something. He has already discerned the best course of action and that is the way it should be done.

His timing is also perfect. We must be careful that we don't try to 'help' God by hastening the results. A little girl had been in the garden for some while and when she came indoors her mother asked what she had been doing. She replied, 'In the garden helping God', and then went on to explain that she had seen a rose almost flowering and had opened it up for God! Of course, in doing this she had spoilt the rose. Beware of 'pushing' God. His timing is perfect.

So, do you want to enter into something that is perfect, something without a fault, something which is perfectly reasonable and that will bring you great satisfaction? If the answer is 'Yes,' as it surely must be, then you must follow the will of God and you will 'prove' it to be just that.

In the Old Testament King David was able to say, 'As for God, his way is perfect; the word of the Lord is flawless. He is a shield for all who take refuge in him . . . It is God who arms me with strength and makes my way perfect' (Psalm 18:30,32).

3. The will of God is pleasing

The word 'pleasing' applies both to me and to God, as we shall see.

Perhaps some of us are afraid to commit ourselves too readily to the prayer, 'Your will be done.' Some years ago a lady remarked on this fact to a Christian friend and said that she was afraid that God might take her little boy or perhaps send some great trial. The wise friend replied, 'Suppose your child should come to you and say, "I want to do just what you want today." Would you then say to yourself, "Now is my opportunity to make my child do all the disagreeable things I want done. I will take advantage of his willingness to please me by cutting off all his pleasure and imposing a hard day on him"?' 'Of course not,' said the mother, 'I would give him the best day I could possibly plan.' 'So,' replied this wise person, 'can you think that God is less just and loving than you are?'

It has been said that 'My deepest happiness and the will of God for my life are synonymous terms', that is, they mean the same thing. If he is a good and perfect God, could his will for my life be anything other than that which would give me the greatest satisfaction?

But I said that the word 'pleasing' applies not only to me but to God himself, and so anything *contrary* to the will of God is likely to have severe repercussions. Robert Haldane writes, 'He approves of nothing but obedience to his own commands.' We must recognize the black and white of this. To be contrary to the will of God is what puts a man under the wrath of God, for we have seen that he cannot be pleased with anything outside of his will. It might *appear* to be good, it might certainly seem harmless humanly speaking, but it is only the doing of his will that God finds pleasing.

We have clearly seen that Jesus was continually doing the will of his Father and more than once he was given the assurance that his Father was well pleased with him (Matthew 3:17; 17:5). We are not to expect an audible voice from heaven commending our obedience, but the Holy Spirit will assure us that we are pleasing God as we prove and test his will.

But to some who are in the middle of pressures and difficulties perhaps Paul's description of God's will can appear to be like 'a red rag to a bull'. 'Good, perfect and pleasing' are not the words you would use at this moment in time to describe God's will.

A personal illustration will perhaps be helpful. A number of years ago I began to suffer severe anxiety symptoms. Preaching was difficult, sleep was irregular and panic was never far away. This was accentuated because neither I nor anyone else could suggest any reason why it should be so. I was experiencing something like the symptoms of a nervous breakdown and yet I was not conscious of any extra pressure which might have brought this about.

The doctors prescribed tranquillizers without any real effect, until eventually it was suggested that I should have some tests at a local hospital. An overactive thyroid was immediately diagnosed; this could be controlled medically and after some weeks of treatment the symptoms subsided. I had been struggling in this situation for almost six months. I am convinced, in looking back on that experience, that there were lessons that I had to learn which were going to be of real value to me in my ministry. It would have been extremely difficult for me to have accepted this experience as the 'good and perfect and pleasing' will of God *at the time*, and yet I see now that this was the way God chose to teach me something I couldn't learn in any other way. Do you see how it is sometimes necessary for us to go right through an experience like that in order that we might fully express our trust in God and also that we might better be able to 'comfort those in any trouble with the comfort we ourselves have received from God'? (2 Corinthians 1:4).

If that is the way God chooses to lead you, it could be an experience that will last for a few hours, days, weeks, months or even years, but trust in him because 'God is faithful; he will not let you be tempted beyond what you can bear. But when you are tempted, he will also

61

provide a way out so that you can stand up under it' (1 Corinthians 10:13). That is a promise!

May he give us the faith to pray in any situation:

> Thy way, not mine, O Lord,
> However dark it be;
> Lead me by Thine own hand,
> Choose Thou the path for me.
>
> Smooth let it be or rough,
> It will be still the best;
> Winding or straight it leads
> Right onward to Thy rest.
>
> Take Thou my cup, and it
> With joy or sorrow fill,
> As best to Thee may seem,
> Choose Thou my good or ill.

4.
Down to brass tacks
The will of God and the way to find it

4.
Down to brass tacks
The will of God and the way to find it

It was a wise man who said, 'To know God's will is man's greatest treasure; to do God's will is life's greatest privilege.'

Knowing and doing the will of God is the distinguishing mark of the believer. The Bible says that 'Those who are led by the Spirit of God are sons of God' (Romans 8:14). A child is led by his parent, a soldier by his officer and Christians by the Spirit of God. Matthew Henry reminds us that we are 'not driven as beasts but led as rational creatures'. Another writer points out that 'only those who are ruled by God's Spirit are reckoned to be His sons. This is the mark by which God acknowledges His own.' Certainly the Bible teaches us that our obedience to God's revealed will shows him that we love him. So, as those who have been privileged to be called into God's family and who have been given 'the right to become children of God', we should want to know *how*, *when* and *where* we can do anything that pleases him. But perhaps we need some help in finding the *way* and that is the purpose of this chapter.

First it must be made clear that there are some matters on which we need no further guidance. Within the Bible there are statements and principles concerning certain matters which are clear for all of us to see.

We know, for instance, that the first thing that is required from any person is that he or she should repent and believe on the Lord Jesus Christ. When men asked Jesus, 'What must we do to do the works God requires?' Jesus answered, 'The work of God is this: to believe in the one he has sent' (John 6:28,29). God will not adapt that first step for anyone.

Then the Bible shows us that for the Christian, sanctification, or holiness, is the will of God. Paul tells us that 'It is God's will that you should be holy' (1 Thessalonians 4:3).

Then it is God's will that Christians should prove their faith by good works. Peter tells us that 'It is God's will that by doing good you should silence the ignorant talk of foolish men' (1 Peter 2:15). All of these are positive statements setting out certain requirements which God has for his children. They are clear for all to see.

There are also negatives that we must beware of. For example, Paul tells us, 'Do not be yoked together with unbelievers. For what do righteousness and wickedness have in common?' (2 Corinthians 6:14). This can have reference to any relationship which requires commitment between the two parties, so though it certainly applies to marriage, it could also apply, for instance, to business life.

Again a Christian believer could never suggest that God is making an exception in his life in guiding him to be dishonest, because that is contrary to the very nature of God.

So, on these and many other subjects we need no further guidance. You will appreciate, therefore, how important it is that we know the Word of God, so that these basic principles become a part of our lives in order that we do those things which please God.

But when we move outside of those basic principles, what then? There are certain areas in which our experience is not straightforward. Individual circumstances are different and God calls people in various ways and to a multiplicity of tasks. All of us find ourselves in this situation at some stage in our lives and it is therefore helpful to have a procedure that can be followed in endeavouring to find out just what God wants us to do in this situation.

Before we begin to look at any procedures, we must firstly consider the preparation that might be necessary in our lives.

1. Preparation for finding the will of God

We have acknowledged that there are some areas in which we can already know God's revealed will and that there are other areas where for each individual person it is a matter of discerning for himself. This can include seemingly trivial matters as well as some of the greatest decisions in our lives. Remember that *both* are important because they are the will of God for our lives.

We must, however, understand that our spiritual condition and attitude to God have a tremendous bearing on this subject. Are we tuned in to God? Is the channel of communication open? Do we make it as easy as possible for God to speak to us?

Waiting to be interviewed for a job as a wireless operator, a group of applicants paid little attention to the sound of dots and dashes which came over the loudspeaker. Suddenly one of them rushed into the employer's office. Soon he returned, smiling.

'I got the job!' he exclaimed.

'How did you get in ahead of us?' the others asked.

'You might have been considered if you had not been so busy talking that you didn't hear the manager's coded message,' he replied. 'It said, "The man I need must always be on the alert. The first one who interprets this and comes directly into my private office will be hired."'

The lesson, of course, is clear. Sometimes we do not hear God's directives because we are not listening for him to speak to us, or even expecting him to speak to us. Never ignore the book through which God has promised to speak to us, his Word, the Bible.

Then what about the attitude of our hearts? A believer and an unbeliever will obviously look at life's decisions in totally different ways and from entirely different standpoints. However, it is possible for two *believers* to look at a situation in alternative ways because of the difference in the attitude of their hearts. It is possible for one to *seek* God's will to obey it and for the other to wait until he knows God's will before deciding whether or not to obey it.

If someone asks me the question, 'Will you do something for me?' basically my answer can be one of three. I can say either, 'Yes', or 'No', or 'Tell me what it is before I decide.' The latter might be a very wise attitude when dealing with fellow human beings, but there is no need for us to act in that way towards God. If it is something that he wills for us we have already acknowledged that it must be for our good, and it is not for us to choose *which* of God's instructions we will obey. That is not a good expression of the relationship which should exist between us and it is sure to bring problems. Remember that delayed obedience is disobedience and disobedience is sin.

This brings us to the fact that any sin in our lives will prove a hindrance to our knowing the will of God. This is very important. The psalmist says, 'If I had cherished sin in my heart, the Lord would not have listened' (Psalm 66:18). The word 'cherished' is the significant word. If we know there is sin in our lives and leave it unconfessed, or if we pretend to be what we are not, or if we relish sin and still seek God's help or guidance in some other direction then he will not listen to us. Our communion with God is broken, we are out of step, we are not in agreement. Any and all sin must mean this because of the holy nature of God. Sin in the believer's life is viewed seriously by him. God does not look at his children through 'rose-tinted spectacles' and allow them more liberty in sin than the unbeliever. Sin in the believer is an abomination and an affront to God, who sent Christ to deliver us from it (See Galatians 1:4).

Perhaps, therefore, this has brought to light some of the preparations you need to make before you are ready to know the next step in God's will for your life. You must deal with this first of all. This very thing is perhaps the next step in the will of God for you right now.

Are you ready to go on? Are you willing to obey, whatever the cost? In a prayer meeting some while ago someone prayed, 'Lord we are afraid to do our own will for fear of the consequences. Teach us your will.' That is the right way to look at the will of God in relation to our own will. Frances Ridley Havergal used to say, 'Once the will of God was a sigh, now it has become a song.' Let us always beware about presupposing that God's will for our lives is sure to be something that we do *not* want. It could and should be the very thing that is in line with our own desires. It has been said that 'The will of God will never take you where the grace of God cannot keep you,' so don't worry!

71

Having looked at the initial preparation that might be necessary, let us now begin to look at the practical steps which we can take.

2. Procedure for finding the will of God

The word 'procedure' should be explained. It would be wrong to imply that there is one particular formula for every situation. However, there are a number of means which God has used to lead his people and it is possible that he will use one, some, or all of these to lead you.

Perhaps it would be helpful if at this point I outline a 'procedure' which has much to commend it.

Here are typical steps which should be considered.

a. We must do all that we can to deal with any hindrance to our hearing and obeying God's voice. Certainly any sin must be confessed and forsaken. We may even have to ask God to make us willing to do his will. God approves of this openness which will lead to oneness with him and so he will do all that is necessary on his part.

At the same time, remember the following important facts.

a. God does not promise short cuts. It may be necessary for us to learn lessons along the way.

b. He does not promise a blueprint for the future. The entire picture will not be laid out for us. Almost always it will be one step at a time.

c. He does not promise feelings, though these must not be ignored. They must, however, be examined very carefully because our physical feelings can affect what is a spiritual decision and if the two are not in harmony, then we will be confused and liable to error.

d. He does not promise signs, though again if they are given they must not be ignored.

If God chooses to lead us in any of these ways, we must be convinced that it is God's leading because the devil can counterfeit and influence signs and circumstances.

In all of this remember to compare what is said or what happens with the Bible. Do not trust anyone's word implicitly, except God's

Word. John warns us, 'Do not believe every spirit, but test the spirits to see whether they are from God' (1 John 4:1). If something is not confirmed by the Word of God then reject it, because without a biblical basis it is either hearsay or heresy.

Here I must underline what is of paramount importance in discerning the will of God, and that is the proper use of prayer and the Word of God, the Bible. Whatever else any Christian might use, he should certainly use the means of grace God has provided for this purpose.

It is vital constantly to bring all of these matters, whether they be large or small, to God in prayer. Prayer is one of the best and loveliest ways in which we can show our dependence on God. Let us come to him often, making sure that we come to pray and not merely to worry in his presence. Much of the time spent in so-called prayer is often time spent trying to sort the problem out for ourselves. That is not the best expression of trust. We must formulate our requests and take them to God. Reminders of the ways in which God has led us in the past will be an encouragement for the future. Paul knew something of this when he encouraged the Philippians not to be anxious about anything, 'but in everything, by prayer and petition, *with thanksgiving,* present your requests to God. And the peace of God, which transcends all understanding, will guide your hearts and minds in Christ Jesus' (Philippians 4:6,7).

Then, of course, if in daily life we ask someone to guide us to a particular destination we must obviously be prepared to listen to their directions. So, in the same way, when we have spoken to God, our daily reading of God's Word will provide our heavenly Guide with a channel for speaking to us. We must come to the Bible with an open mind and heart, prepared to receive his word for our situation at the time. We must try to avoid looking for verses which we think will fit our circumstances. This can be very dangerous. We must be patient and wait for God, so that when he speaks we shall know. There is nothing like the thrill of being convinced that God has spoken as one verse or phrase lights up for us. From that moment on, there should be no doubt in our minds about that particular course of action.

But I believe that there is still one thing that needs to be said. It is possible to explore all of these avenues and still to be unconvinced as to the step that we must take. This will inevitably bring anxiety and perhaps even panic. What we are going to look at now is

77

often either ignored or forgotten, and yet I believe it to be vital to the way in which we approach this subject. It is rooted firmly and squarely in the character of God.

3. Patience in finding the will of God

We noticed earlier that God promises to guide us (Psalm 25:9), but what we did not examine were the conditions under which God is able to guide. 'He guides the humble in what is right and teaches them his way. All the ways of the Lord are loving and faithful for those who keep the demands of his covenant . . . Who, then, is the man that fears the Lord? He will instruct him in the way chosen for him' (Psalm 25:9—12). Notice the relationship of this person to God. He is *'humble'*, that is, he is submissive and willing to be led. He is *obedient* for he 'keep[s] the demands of his covenant'. Therefore it is *that* person who will be instructed in 'the way chosen for him'.

Providing, therefore, there is nothing on *our* side to hinder God leading us, then the greatest comfort and assurance we can have in the matter of finding the will of God is that in some way, because God is God, he is going to make it clear to us. On the one hand, there is a loving Father who wants to lead us because that is why he redeemed us. He is also one who has promised to lead us and who is quite capable of leading us. All of that is because he is God. On the other hand, here is the one who is the child of God wanting to know God's will and in a condition to hear his voice. With such a relationship existing, it is not possible for us to fail to find the way that God wants us to go. We may even think that we are slow to learn and not terribly bright; God understands that because he made us, and it is no problem for him to reveal his will to us — in his own time! If we have reached this point and still experience anxiety then the probable cause is that of impatience!

The psalmist makes this so clear when he tells us, 'Be still before the Lord and wait patiently for him' (Psalm 37:7). Or again, 'Commit your way to the Lord; trust in him' (Psalm 37:5).

The writer of the Proverbs encourages us to 'trust in the Lord with all your heart and lean not on your own understanding; in all your ways acknowledge him, and he will make your paths straight' (Proverbs 3:5,6). Isn't that helpful? 'Trust and wait patiently', says God. It is not always as easy as it sounds, yet it is *the* way to be at peace in the matter of guidance. Here is a way in which our faith in God is really going to be tested. Are we prepared for that? What an example that is going to be to those around us, and what a strengthening to our faith when, in his own time, God proves yet again that 'he is faithful'!

George Müller, who ran an orphanage for God in Bristol, said, 'I never remember in all my Christian course that I ever sincerely and patiently sought to know the will of God by the teaching of the Holy Ghost, through the instrumentality of the Word of God, but I have always been rightly directed. But if honesty of heart and uprightness before God were lacking, or if I did not patiently wait upon God for instruction, or if I preferred the counsel of my fellow men to the declarations of the Word of God, I made great mistakes.'

Paul, in writing to the Ephesian Christians, encourages them to make 'the most of every opportunity'. He did not, however, leave that as good advice with no practical way of carrying it out. His advice to them, in order that they might make the best use of the time, was to 'understand what the Lord's will is' (Ephesians 5:16,17). Do the will of God — that is the perfect use of our time. Someone has rightly said that 'Out of God's will there can be no success; whereas in his will there can be no failure.'

So ask God what he wants you to do, patiently wait for his answer and then do it! Remember that 'To know God's will is man's greatest treasure; to do God's will is his greatest privilege.'

5.
A final word
The will of God and its consequences

5.
A final word
The will of God and its consequences

Some consider God to be little more than a martinet, a strict disciplinarian. This is understandable on their part, since these people are usually among those who know little or nothing of the character of God and therefore the very idea of having to obey someone they cannot see and do not appear to need is foolish. However, knowledge of the Word of God and an experience which has revealed something of the character of God make it absolutely clear to us that God does not require his will to be done merely because he likes to see his creatures 'jump to it', or that all he requires for his own pleasure are mere puppets. There is a very real purpose behind the will of God, which, if we embrace it, will not only bring glory to him, but blessing to the obedient. Throughout human history, man has run into problems whenever he has stepped outside of the moral guidelines provided for him by an all-wise God.

How many of the problems in society today are brought about because laws have been disregarded? How many problems in family life exist because parents' guidelines are either ignored or perhaps were never there in the first place? But, most important of all, how many problems in the believer's spiritual life are there for the very same reason? There has been disobedience to the will of God.

I have had the privilege of counselling many Christian people who knew that something was wrong in their spiritual lives but didn't know what it was or why it was there. Very often during our conversation they became aware of some disobedience which had never been confessed and forgiven. They hadn't realized that this very thing was a hindrance to their spiritual growth. Spiritual blessing in our own lives is linked inseparably with obedience. God said to the Israelites, '*If* you obey me fully and keep my covenant *then* out of all nations you will be my treasured possession' (Exodus 19:5). God said to Solomon, '*If* you walk in my ways and obey my statutes and commands as David your father did, I will give

you a long life' (1 Kings 3:14). The Bible says
that 'The Lord's love is with those who fear
him, and his righteousness with their children's
children — with those who keep his covenant
and remember to obey his precepts' (Psalm
103:17,18). Jesus said, '*If* you obey my commands, you will remain in my love, just as
I have obeyed my Father's commands and
remain in his love.' He also said, 'You are my
friends *if* you do what I command' (John
15:10,14). Jesus said, 'Now that you know
these things, you will be blessed *if* you do
them' (John 13:17).

But, as well as blessing enjoyed in this life,
there will be *eternal* repercussions from either
obeying or disobeying the will of God.

In one of his parables, Jesus emphasizes the
importance of doing the will of God as it is
revealed to us. He tells the story of a master
who during his absence left his servant in charge
of all his possessions. The servant did not fulfil
his obligations and the master returned at a
time when he was least expected. Jesus said,
'That servant who knows his master's will
and does not get ready or does not do what
his master wants will be beaten with many
blows. But the one who does not know and
does things deserving punishment will be beaten
with few blows. From everyone who has been

given much, much will be demanded; and from the one who has been entrusted with much, much more will be asked' (Luke 12:47, 48). God is not unjust to punish in the same way those who don't do his will because they didn't know it. But God's people are supposed to know his will and we are without excuse if, knowing it, we disobey.

If there is retribution for disobedience, then there is most certainly a reward for obedience. The writer to the Hebrews says, 'You need to persevere so that when you have done the will of God, you will receive what he has promised' (Hebrews 10:36). Here was an encouragement to persecuted Christians to persevere. In the following chapter the writer gives his readers examples of those who persevered in their faith. 'Look, it can be done!' he is saying. The reward that is referred to is 'the promise' or 'what he has promised'. What is this?

It is mentioned earlier in the letter. 'Christ is the mediator of a new covenant, that those who are called may receive the promised eternal inheritance' (Hebrews 9:15). These Jewish Christians would be reminded of their fore-fathers who had received their earthly inheritance — the land of Canaan — and now they are promised something eternal of which Canaan is the type, or the picture.

Peter, writing to Christians in similar circumstances, reminds them of 'an inheritance that can never perish, spoil or fade — kept in heaven for you' (1 Peter 1:4). We can see that this inheritance is not exposed to defilement from outside or decay from within, neither will it waste or wear away and it is kept in heaven for us. The Bible speaks of us having the 'earnest', or the guarantee, of the complete reward, in the person of the Holy Spirit, who lives within us: 'You were marked in him with a seal, the promised Holy Spirit, who is a deposit guaranteeing our inheritance' (Ephesians 1:13, 14). The 'earnest' or deposit was the first instalment of goods from an agreement entered into by two tradesmen. The Spirit of God in us is the first instalment of a heavenly inheritance which makes the payment of the remainder obligatory. We have just a foretaste of what is to come as we persevere in doing the will of God.

And there is one thing more. John says, 'The world and its desires pass away, but the man who does the will of God lives for ever' (1 John 2:17). Here are the alternatives. We have noticed that the characteristic of the world is that it does not do the will of God and John confirms in the previous verse: 'For everything in the world, the cravings of sinful man, the lust of his eyes and the boasting of what he has and does — comes not from the Father but from the world' (1 John 2:16) and all of this is going to pass away. But notice that the man who does the will of God 'lives for ever'. This is the great alternative — loving the world or doing the will of God. The world is transient and passing; God's will and the one who obeys it are eternal. No wonder, therefore, that John said, 'Do not love the world or anything in the world. If anyone loves the world, the love of the Father is not in him' (1 John 2:15).

We often refer to the fact that as Christians we must leave this world. There is a truth in that because the Bible teaches a 'leaving behind'. We are strangers and pilgrims on earth and citizens of heaven. But it is important to notice here that it is the world that is going and we are staying! We are the proprietors and we have a right to stay if we do the will of God. The world has forfeited its title. All things are ours!

These then are some of the consequences following our response to what God requires from us. God promises us something that our finite minds cannot grasp. What have we done to deserve it? Nothing at all. What we deserve is retribution. What we are going to receive is a reward!

Above all we can look forward to the day when our prayer will be answered and his will will be 'done on earth as it is in heaven'.

Other books from

EVANGELICAL PRESS

HOW TO ENJOY YOUR BIBLE

John Blanchard

John Blanchard believes that Christians are meant to **enjoy** the Bible, and that reading the Scriptures should be an exciting adventure into God's truth and purposes for our lives.

So how can we **enjoy** God's Word and avoid the trap of our Bible study being a dull, boring duty? In this excellent book, the author, an internationally known preacher and evangelist, shows us how this can be achieved.

"Simple, vivid, accurate, warm, practical and searching, it is all that we have come to expect of its author."

J. I. Packer

"It is ideally written for the young convert, has much to teach the mature Christian and is suitable for Bible study groups of every kind."

Rev. Kenneth Paterson

WHAT IN THE WORLD IS A CHRISTIAN?

John Blanchard

In these days of religious confusion many people are asking, 'What in the world is a Christian? Because of a lack of teaching, or a superficial approach to Scripture, or a restless chasing after mystical 'experiences' they are unable to give an adequate answer to this question. In this revised edition of his book, John Blanchard attempts to do so. The author is convinced that there is no substitute for straightforward biblical teaching in order to produce healthy, balanced and progressive Christians.

"For the person who has never discovered Christian faith, for the early disciple in doctrine, for the mature Christian, and for the one who reads for both pleasure and profit, this book is a must."

The Harvester

NOW THAT I'M A CHRISTIAN

E. F. Kevan

Becoming a Christian is just the beginning of a
new way of life. The new believer needs help to
understand and put into practice the basic
teaching of the Bible. This book has been written
with a view to meeting that need.

This is a book which can be confidently placed in
the hands of those who are young in the faith. It
will be found invaluable either for private study
or as a basis for group study or discussions.

DIALOGUE WITH GOD

Guy Appéré

What is prayer? Why do we pray? How should we pray? What about those prayers which appear to remain unanswered? How can we know if we are praying according to God's will?

These and many similar questions are answered in a thoughtful and practical way by Guy Appéré, an experienced pastor. He conveys something of the wonder of this unique relationship between man and God, this **Dialogue with God** which occupies such a vital place in the Christian life and which is so essential for happy fulfilment in that life.